Original title:
Running Late to the Meaning of Life

Copyright © 2025 Creative Arts Management OÜ
All rights reserved.

Author: Henry Beaumont
ISBN HARDBACK: 978-1-80566-031-6
ISBN PAPERBACK: 978-1-80566-326-3

Unseen Journeys and Wandering Spirits

In a race with a clock that ticks too fast,
I trip on my laces, oh, what a blast!
Coffee spills down, I laugh through the mess,
Chasing life's secrets, I must confess.

The bus zooms by, who knew it would flee?
I wave with a smile, just me and my glee.
Maps in my pocket, directions unclear,
But hey, what's an adventure without a bit of cheer?

I meet a lost cat that's stuck in a tree,
"We're both in the wrong place," it seems to agree.
We marvel at squirrels, both laughing away,
Life's silly moments make up for the fray.

With every missed turn, a new story spins,
Like forgetting to pack my favorite wins.
Yet joy in the chaos bursts forth like a song,
In unseen journeys, I finally belong.

Daisies in the Path of Minutes

Oh, clock, you tease with your tick-tock laugh,
As I trip on thoughts, I lose my path.
My coffee's cold, my toast's on the floor,
Yet here I stand, wanting just one more.

With daisies sprouting from lost time's seams,
I stumble on while chasing dreams.
Each moment's dance, a quirky feat,
As I chase the day away on two left feet.

The Weight of Unread Pages

A stack of books that I dare not crack,
Each title whispers, 'Hey, don't hold back!'
Like bricks they sit, with dust on their spines,
I joke and laugh, 'Oh, they're like fine wines!'

I'd rather scroll through memes and scrolls,
Than dive into worlds where the plot unfolds.
Yet still I ponder what lies inside,
As I juggle my snacks and my thoughts collide.

Harmonies of the Overlooked

In chaos of noise, a symphony sings,
Yet here I am, missing all the strings.
Birds are chirping their sweet serenade,
But I'm stuck in traffic, feeling delayed.

Whispers of laughter flutter around,
As I waltz through life, never quite sound.
Onlookers glance, but I'm in a trance,
With my coffee cup doing the dizzy dance.

A Symphony of Missed Chances

With every 'oops' and 'whoops' that fly,
I write my story and wonder why.
A missed turn here, a blink and a sigh,
The best laid plans just say goodbye.

Yet in the hiccups, joy's little prance,
Turns fumbles to giggles, life's silly dance.
So I'll raise my toast to the chaos I meet,
In this merry-go-round of skipped heartbeat.

The Quiet in the Commotion

Amidst the honks and shouts galore,
I trip and fall, then rise once more.
With coffee spilled and hair askew,
I chase the day that runs from view.

The bus I missed, a dance I made,
While people glared, my plans betrayed.
But life's a laugh, a silly game,
In chaos, joy lights up the flame.

Searching for Stillness in Motion

A marathon of socks and shoes,
I search for peace, but what's the use?
My watch insists, so off I fly,
Yet stop to watch a butterfly.

I juggle tasks in frantic haste,
But there's no time for mindful taste.
So here I go, arms full of stuff,
Who knew this life would be so tough?

When Time Winks at You

Each tick and tock, a little tease,
I step on toes and bump some knees.
Yet time, it winks, with playful glee,
"Chill out, my friend, just let it be."

I dash through puddles, slip and slide,
A merry dance where chaos hides.
With laughter ringing in my ears,
I'll find my way through giggles and tears.

The Last Breath of Yesterday

Yesterday's plans, they run amok,
Like socks that hide in laundry's flock.
I chase the sun, it sets too fast,
As time slips by, a laughing cast.

With every step, a little blunder,
I trip on thoughts, my mind in thunder.
But still I grin, oh what a sight,
For life's a joke, and that feels right!

Navigating Time's Relentless Current

I tripped on the clock, it laughed and spun,
Chasing my dreams like a troublesome run.
The future waved back from its distant shore,
While I fumbled and stumbled, yelling, "More!"

A donut break here, a nap over there,
Life's marathon feels like a comedy fair.
I search for the wisdom hiding like mice,
In cupboards of chaos, and seconds of spice.

The Urgency of Unspoken Truths

Time whispers softly, "Let's pick up the pace,"
While I'm busy tripping on my shoelace.
Answers all giggle as they dance just out of reach,
Waving their hands like they want to teach.

With every missed train, there's a new joke told,
About plans I once had, now just gathering mold.
Like misplacing my keys and then losing my mind,
I chase after sanity, but it's hard to find.

Footsteps on the Edge of Epiphany

I tiptoe on sidewalks of bright neon dreams,
With squirrels critiquing my life's wild schemes.
They point at the post-it notes fluttering by,
And giggle at wisdom I can't seem to spy.

Every corner I turn feels like a dance,
With life's little riddles, I never get a chance.
The enlightenment train is late to the gate,
And I'm still in line for a slice of fate.

The Prelude to Self-Discovery

In a world full of hurry, I dawdle and spin,
While wisdom does cartwheels, grinning wide with a grin
I pull at the strings of my tangled-up thoughts,
Like a cat with a yarn ball, lost in their knots.

Searching for answers buried deep in a laugh,
While fate scribbles jokes on a whimsical path.
Each moment a puzzle that's all dressed in flair,
I dance as I ponder the meaning laid bare.

Balancing on a Narrow Brink

I dashed past the baker, lost my hat,
Chasing time like a chihuahua in a spat.
Juggling life like a clumsy clown,
Fell in a puddle, splashed the town.

The toaster popped, my breakfast flew,
I'd catch the bus, but the dog just chewed.
Life's a circus, a show gone wrong,
Yet here I am, singing my song.

The Clockwork of Dreams

Tick-tock, the clock mocks my race,
Dreams are tangled in a scarf I misplaced.
With socks unmatched and hair stuck out,
I'm fashionably late—without a doubt.

The rooster crows, but I've missed the dawn,
Chased my thoughts like a runaway fawn.
In this madcap tango, I twirl and spin,
Trying to find where my time begins.

When the World Stood Still

A pause, a blink, the world hit 'snooze',
I spilled my coffee, wearing my blues.
The cat pinched my chair, claimed it first,
While I dodge duties, oh, I'm cursed!

Every moment's a jigsaw piece,
Missing edges, seeking peace.
Hiding in laughter, I embrace the fun,
Waiting for that afternoon sun.

Unraveled Threads of Time

My clock's a liar, its hands play tricks,
Tying my shoelaces in a mix.
Spinning like tops, my thoughts take flight,
Seeking the meaning, lost in the night.

With wrinkles in plans and hiccups in lines,
I dance through the chaos, sipping on wines.
Life's a riddle with a punchline I chase,
Stumbling through the cosmic race.

Echoing Heartbeats of Resolve

In a rush with mismatched shoes,
I stumble over yesterday's clues.
Heartbeats echo, a comical race,
Chasing dreams in a frenzied pace.

Laughter spills from my flailing glee,
As life unveils its bright mystery.
Tickling thoughts with a wink and a grin,
Finding joy in the chaos within.

An awkward dash under the street light,
Stars giggle, urging me to take flight.
Fate is a jester, a playful guide,
In this mad dash, let humor abide.

So I run with my heart like a drum,
Mixing life's key with my own silly hum.
The journey is messy, a joyous spree,
Living each moment, wild and free.

A Detour into Clarity

I took a wrong turn at the corner of fate,
Where questions are served on a laughable plate.
Maps are for sages, but I'm just a clown,
Stumbling through life, can't keep my crown.

A detour leads to a curious sight,
Potatoes in tutus, dancing with might.
My thoughts start to bubble, like soda pop fizz,
In a world where nonsense is all that there is.

Embrace the bananas, the circus bouquet,
The answers I seek are just games that we play.
Life whispers secrets in riddles and rhymes,
As I leap over puddles of silly good times.

So here's to the wanderers, lost on their quest,
Finding clarity when chaos is best.
With giggles and grins, my heart starts to sing,
In this carnival of living, I've found my wing.

The Starlit Path Untraveled

Under the stars, I missed the right route,
Tripping on laughter while giving a hoot.
The moon winks down with a glimmering smile,
Inviting me in for a whimsical mile.

I dance with shadows, I twirl with the breeze,
In a cosmic ballet, I'm doing as I please.
Life's puzzle pieces are scrambled around,
But maybe the fun is what I have found.

Through the darkness, I chase after jokes,
Chasing bright comets and friendly clokes.
Dreams play hide and seek in the night,
In woods full of wonders, I'm taking a bite.

So come, let's wander, no map in our hand,
With giggles and prancing, we'll make our stand.
If I miss the destination, that's perfectly fine,
For the starlit path is completely divine.

Between Tick and Tock

In the land of clocks, I twirl and prance,
Forget the seconds, let's start a dance.
Tick tock tickles, the minutes lose track,
With a grin on my face, there's no looking back.

Days jump like bunnies, hopping away,
While I chase the giggles that lead me to play.
I've got a pocketful of whimsical time,
Count all the chuckles, they curl like a rhyme.

Each tick is a giggle, each tock is a cheer,
As I race through the nonsense, I hold it so dear.
With each moment I find, I collect all the fun,
In the zany chaos, I'm bright as the sun.

So here's to the journey, the dance of the clock,
Life's clock may be silly, but I'm ready to rock.
With laughter as fuel, I embrace every tick,
Between tick and tock, I find my own trick.

A Dance with the Clock

Tick tock, I'm in a race,
Chasing moments, what a face!
Coffee spills, my shirt is stained,
Life's a stage where I'm untrained.

Time winks at me with a grin,
I stumble, trip, and then I spin.
The clock laughs, it never waits,
I'm late for life, but what's the fate?

Pigeons scatter, I dart around,
In a whirl, I haven't found.
The secret's in the frantic glee,
Embracing chaos, wild and free.

So here I am, no grand parade,
Just jumbled thoughts that won't cascade.
With every tick, I twist and shout,
Time's a dance, there's joy, no doubt.

The Subtle Urgency of Now

A coffee shop, my heart's delight,
Where people rush, but I'm polite.
I sip so slow, the world blurs by,
Maybe I'll take the scenic sky.

The urgent folks with charts in hand,
I wonder if they planned and planned.
But here I'm lost in latte art,
Finding meaning's quite the sport.

Look! A bird flies by so free,
I laugh, they're late too, you see?
Moments missed all around, yet,
In this odd pause, I'm not upset.

So I'll cherish time that seems to flee,
In every sip, there's clarity.
Each second's pulse, a gentle nod,
In this now, I feel like God.

Threads of Serendipity

Oh look, I lost my left shoe,
But found a penny, that will do!
Life's little quirks, absurdly grand,
Stitching fate with a clumsy hand.

On buses late, with mismatched socks,
I laugh at time's confusing clocks.
Each mishap's just a silly fate,
Dancing through this wobbly state.

A donut shop with sprinkles bright,
I take a bite, it feels so right.
What I thought was lost in space,
Is found again, in sweet embrace.

So let's toast to every stumble,
To happy fails and joyful jumble.
In this grand quilt of chaos spun,
Finding meaning is half the fun.

Delayed Revelations

I woke up late, the sun is high,
My dreams were rich, but my pants are dry.
In a rush, I miss the plot,
Should've listened to my gut, not thought.

Chasing wisdom on a hurry train,
The conductor's lost, must be insane.
Questions swirl as time flies past,
Delayed insights, that's my cast.

The guru on the corner smiled,
But I sped by, a whirlwind child.
Was that a clue or just a sneeze?
In this chaos, I'll just breathe.

So here I laugh at cosmic signs,
Every detour twists and aligns.
Life's punchlines spring from the mess,
Delayed cheers, I still feel blessed.

The Art of Being Fashionably Late

I left the house at half past five,
Wore mismatched socks, oh what a vibe.
The party starts at eight, you say?
I'll waltz in like it's 'haute' today.

My hair was flat, my shoes don't shine,
Yet in my mind, I feel divine.
Tick-tock sings a silly song,
And yet I stroll; it can't be wrong.

The cake was cut, the punch is poured,
I missed the dance, but here's my chord:
A laugh, a joke, they can't be late,
With every step, I own my fate.

So here's my flair, my vibrant state,
To arrive in style, the perfect bait.
When others fret, I take my chance,
With every late arrival, I still dance.

When Time Stumbles

Clock's hands spinning like a top,
I chase my thoughts but time won't stop.
Coffee's cold, but I feel warm,
As I fumble through this daily swarm.

The bus arrives—wait, is it mine?
I run a race with no finish line.
In flip-flops now, I glance around,
With each misstep, joy is found.

Lost my keys? Now there's a shock,
I greet the world, what a fine clock!
Minutes run wild, like dogs unleashed,\nBut every laugh brings sweet release.

Smile spread wide, I must confess,
Life's not a test, it's just a mess.
So when I'm late, I shake my head,
And dance my way to my own thread.

Lost in the Haste

Rushing through the crowded street,
Tripped on air, feel the heat.
Glancing at my watch, oh dear!
It's already past the half-past cheer.

Dodging puddles, almost slipped,
My morning toast, I surely skipped.
Every corner turned, a brand new task,
In this wild race, I barely bask.

The world zooms by, a colorful blur,
A little chaos—oh, what a spur!
Stumbling jokes and laughter loud,
I blend in with this bustling crowd.

But when I drop my bag and sigh,
A friendly wave says goodbye.
In this mad rush, I find my place,
Chasing joy in the frantic race.

The Journey Without a Map

Off I trot without a clue,
Wondering where the path goes too.
With snacks in hand and shoes askew,
Life's a puzzle, let's accrue.

Lost again, but that's the thrill,
Every detour gives a chill.
With laughter sprouting from my heart,
Each wrong turn is a work of art.

Hello, new friends with crazy tales,
Trading stories, plotting trails.
The map was wrong, but oh so right,
In this jumble, I find delight.

So here's my compass, it spins and sways,
Leading me through this quirky maze.
In every laugh and silly blunder,
I'll find my way, no need for wonder.

The Final Stretch of Understandings

I raced with gravity pulling my shoes,
A start line marked by yesterday's snooze.
Thought I'd catch up, but then I saw,
Life's a jest with a cosmic flaw.

Laughter echoes in the late parade,
As wisdom waits in the sunshade.
I missed the bus to self-discovery,
Now I ride the train of mild recovery.

My sneakers squeaked on the path of chance,
Each step a tango, a clumsy dance.
With every breath, I trip and fall,
Life's absurd, but isn't that the call?

So here I stand, in a comedy's light,
Chasing meanings, left and right.
Maybe the secret is found in the chase,
With a chuckle, I embrace the race.

An Overture of Delayed Realizations

Woke up late, found my coffee cold,
Rushed to the stage, missed the script told.
With mismatched socks and hair askew,
An overture plays, but I'm not in view.

Clowns in the audience chuckle loud,
As I fumble through life's chaotic crowd.
My epiphanies come in fits and starts,
Like a juggler dropping all of his parts.

In the spotlight of awkward delays,
I dance through the confusion of wrong ways.
Why do I chase what's rightfully mine?
When all I need is a punchline divine.

So let the curtains rise on this clumsy show,
Where hidden gems of laughter flow.
With every giggle, I clap in delight,
Finding joy in the stumbles of life's flight.

Chasing Shadows of Time

I chased my shadow, thought it was wise,
But it twisted away with a cheeky surprise.
Ticking clocks giggle while I run around,
In their endless mocking, no solace is found.

Sunset arrives like a clumsy friend,
Slipping on life's lessons that never end.
I glance at the watch, it's paused on a grin,
Reminds me that time's my buddy, not kin.

Each hour a joke, every minute a pun,
Life's serendipity, just trying to have fun.
While my brain races, the heart takes a seat,
In this zany race, I admit my defeat.

So I'll linger in laughter, let shadows play,
As I savor each moment, the silly way.
For in the chase of whimsy and rhyme,
I find joy in the ebb of the tick-tock time.

The Clock's Gentle Whisper

The clock whispers secrets, but I've got no ear,
Busy with chaos, it starts to sneer.
Tick-tock chuckles, mocking my haste,
As I miss the bus of profound taste.

Each second a riddle, a giggle disguised,
While I scramble for wisdom, a prize in my eyes.
But the clock taps its face, 'Oh, what a sight!'
A slapstick expression on a stubborn night.

My watch takes a break, has coffee with fate,
While I twirl like a dancer, now far too late.
In the ballet of time, I slip on a shoe,
Oh, what's the hurry? I ask, too anew.

So I'll pause with a laugh, let moments unfold,
With each gentle tick, precious stories retold.
In the symphony of life, join the bright choir,
For in late realizations, we find true desire.

Tumbling Toward Tomorrow

Woke up this morning, forgot my shoe,
Chasing the clock like it's chasing me too.
Coffee's on fire, toast is in flight,
Maybe tomorrow, I'll get it all right.

Legs that are flailing, a laugh on the way,
The dog steals my bagel, what more can I say?
I trip on my thoughts as I tumble and sway,
Life's a wild ride, come dance in the fray.

Maps in my pocket, but none will agree,
My GPS says I'm lost in a tree.
Racing through traffic, a waltz with the fate,
Singing my tune while I'm sealing my fate.

But hey, what is time, if not a grand jest?
Each tick that I miss, puts my patience to test.
So here's to the chaos, the laughter, the run,
Tumbling toward tomorrow, we'll still have our fun.

The Puzzle of Purpose

A box full of pieces, with colors so bright,
Trying to make sense, but it's quite a sight.
Corners and edges, I'm all out of luck,
Diving for answers, but I'm stuck in the muck.

Life's like a jigsaw, with missing parts,
Looking for wisdom in shops selling tarts.
Begin with a corner, oh wait, what's this?
The cat's got the pieces; a moment of bliss.

Puzzles in cafes, with coffee and cake,
It's hard to make sense when you're lost in the wake.
Am I upside down, or the puzzle is wrong?
Maybe I'm just where the pieces belong.

A chuckle escapes as I piece it all through,
Life's a big game, and I'm just passing too.
So, gather your fragments, hear the laughter around,
The puzzle of purpose is joy that's profound.

When Every Second Counts

The door's swinging wide, here comes my parade,
With seconds like popcorn, I'm chasing the shade.
Plans go out the window, like socks in the wash,
Hurry! Oh hurry! But not at a squash!

Grabbed waffles for breakfast, a bite of some glee,
The cat's on the counter; she's eyeing my spree.
Missed the first bus, oh what a great start,
Every tick-tock dances, it's a race with my heart.

Tickle the clock, it's a comical spree,
Why do I pressure? It's just me, not a spree.
Running in circles, the lost and the found,
When every second counts, let laughter abound.

Flip on the radio, tune into the fun,
Every hour's a bonus, and life's a wild run.
So here's to the chaos, the juggling act,
When every second counts, let's make a new pact.

Awakening the Dreamer Within

Stumbling out of slumber, dreams scattered like leaves,
Chasing my thoughts 'neath those pesky old eaves.
Dare I find magic in messes I've made?
The dreamer within me is never dismayed.

Sock puppets dancing, in shades of the day,
Whispering secrets the sunlight would say.
I'll step on a cloud, or I might just take flight,
With whimsy as fuel, I'll soar through the night.

Life's a charade, a colorful play,
With laughter and glitter, we'll dance through the fray.
Awaken the dreamer; let bright colors spin,
In life's grand adventure, we'll always win.

So come, grab your cap, let's chase down the sun,
With giggles and sparkles, we're never done.
Awakening dreamers, we're wild and we're free,
In this wacky old world, just be you and be me.

Elusive Clockwork

Tick-tock, the hands they spin,
Chasing shadows, where to begin?
Coffee spills, a mad dash,
Life's parade, we sprint past fast.

Spare a thought for the slowpoke,
While I fumble with my joke,
Time forgets, it plays a prank,
Lost in thoughts, I fall from rank.

Yet giggles echo in the race,
As I trip, I find my place,
Life's too short to fret and scold,
Let's just laugh and share the gold!

Clock hands laugh, they tease their prey,
While I fumble on this fray,
Can't catch time, must learn to groove,
In this chaos, I will move.

Beyond the Hourglass

Sand slips through the glass so clear,
I rush and slip, yet have no fear,
Awkward dance, a funny fate,
Stumbling headlong, but feeling great.

Panic strikes, oh where's my phone?
Lost the way, I'm on my own,
Yet laughter bubbles like fine wine,
Let's forget the rush, it's fine!

Chasing dreams like a headless duck,
Time's a jester—oh what luck!
Crammed in life's chaotic game,
I wear my wits like a comedy name.

So here I stand, a hero's take,
Not on a path, but in a quake,
Beyond the glass, my sanity sways,
Maybe life's just a joke that plays!

Moments That Slip Away

I run with shoes two sizes small,
Tripping often, I take a fall,
Moments wink and then they flee,
Catch me if you can, oh me!

Chasing after trivia so bright,
Fumbling thoughts in morning light,
Juggling jokes as time runs thin,
In this madness, can I grin?

Time presents its finest jest,
While I ponder what is best,
Missed the bus, missed the show,
But in mischief, joy will grow.

So here I stand, my hair a mess,
Stuck in fun, in all this stress,
While seconds flee like soap in hand,
I'll laugh and dance, and make a stand.

The Last Train to Clarity

On the platform, a whistle blows,
Missed my chance, but who really knows?
All aboard for goofy rides,
Waving bye to my anxious sides.

Thoughts like trains that won't align,
Running late, yet still divine,
In the chaos, there's a style,
Time is silly—let's just smile!

Arriving at a station late,
With a grin upon my fate,
Clarity hides in tangled tracks,
But laughter's train? It never lacks.

So here I stand, just me and fate,
In this mad rush, let's celebrate,
Oh, the journey's what we'll toast,
With a chuckle, here's my boast!

The Beauty of a Missed Connection

I dashed towards the bus, oh what a sight,
But it left without me, what a fright!
I waved my arms, like a crazy dove,
While folks just laughed, but that's how I love.

A pigeon cooed as I chased my fate,
He seemed quite wise, though he was late.
Missed my chance, but here's the twist,
I made a friend, can't resist this list!

The phone rang once, then fell on mute,
Life's punchlines come in a stinky boot.
I'll stroll on paths that are half-designed,
To find the chuckles that I left behind.

So here's to the folly, the laughs we share,
Finding joy in the chaos, in the crazy air.
Each missed connection is a chance to smile,
I'll chase those dreams, though it takes a while.

A Breath Between Two Worlds

I thought I'd leap, but tripped on a shoe,
Life's a dance with steps that skew.
That breath I took, oh what a pause,
Left me wondering about the cause.

In between the clocks, I found some time,
Ticking slowly, like a jolly rhyme.
I spun around, lost in the quest,
Forgot my keys, but I feel so blessed.

The sandwich shop told me to "hurry up,"
But my heart just wanted to fill a cup.
Between the bites, I pondered away,
The essence of joy found in every day.

A moment caught, like a butterfly's wing,
Fluttering softly, does happiness sing?
I breathe in deep, that's where I'll stay,
Finding meaning in this silly ballet.

Whispers from an Open Door

The door creaked wide as I charged right in,
And faced a room filled with polite grins.
"Is this the party? Or did I misread?"
I laughed aloud, fulfilling my need.

A cat on the table, presiding with flair,
Looked at my entrance, gave me a stare.
"Fancy some fish or a slice of cheese?"
I aimed for a chat, but landed with ease.

The punchline hit like a gust of wind,
I told a tale, and everyone grinned.
In total confusion, we shared a cheer,
Laughter erupted; I found my sphere.

So here's to the chaos, the fun that we steal,
From moments unplanned, that make life real.
Whispers of joy from that open door,
Crop up with mishaps, forevermore.

The Mirage of Tomorrow

Tomorrow's dreams danced far away,
I chased like a child in a sunny play.
But time giggled, wearing a sneaky mask,
As I searched for meaning, a challenging task.

With each step forward, I slipped on a joke,
Life's like a clown that never spoke.
"Look over there!" my friends shout out,
Yet I'm still lost in this funny bout.

The mirage shimmered, taunting my gaze,
Promises wrapped in a whimsical haze.
I stumbled through thoughts like a bumpy road,
Gathering laughs as my funny code.

So here's to the twists and the turns we make,
In pursuit of the light, let's have some cake!
Tomorrow may wait, but today's our stage,
Let's embrace the absurd, it's an eternal page.

The Pulse of Yesterday's Echo

In search of wisdom, I made my way,
But coffee spills led my thoughts astray.
I danced with my shoes on the wrong feet,
Chasing shadows in a fun little beat.

The clock's hands spun, like a hamster wheel,
I waved at planes; it felt surreal.
I found my keys up in a tree,
Life's punchline tickled, oh how it flees.

Questions bounced like balls on a lawn,
Answers crawled out like a lazy dawn.
I yelled, 'Wait up!' to my own reflection,
It shrugged and said, 'Next year's election!'

With a map that had only doodles and stars,
I rode my lessons like shiny cars.
So here I stand, lost and yet sly,
Chasing echoes that giggle and fly.

Time Travelers and Wanderers

The past is a buffet where I stuffed my face,
Time travelers whisper, 'Slow down the race!'
I pushed the pedal to get ahead,
But tripped on my laces, and whoops! I fled.

I entered a bar, fancy drinks on the shelf,
I laughed with a mirror; it looked like myself.
The bartender served me a slice of the day,
I sipped on my thoughts—then they flew away.

A portal opened from my kitchen sink,
I took a leap, but it made me rethink.
Reality cracked like old shellac,
I popped right through; I just can't go back.

So here in this cosmos, I joke and I lark,
I'm dodging the signs, I'm missing the mark.
Perhaps in a galaxy far far away,
My answers are hiding, in silly play.

The Long Road to Understanding

I took a trip down the avenue of thought,
Sipped on some wisdom, but I got caught.
A traffic jam of dreams and schemes,
Life's GPS? It's glitchy, it seems.

I asked a squirrel for directions clear,
He chattered and scampered, 'I don't live here!'
Threw breadcrumbs to chase a train of thought,
I was too busy; the lesson was naught.

Wisdom flickered like a neon sign,
It giggled at me through bubbles and brine.
I waved my arms, trying to explain,
Only to find it was all in vain.

So I marched on, with a grin on my face,
Collecting the quirks of this madcap race.
The road may be long, with no end in sight,
But laughter and folly make it feel just right.

Tripped Up by Life's Curriculum

In the school of life, I missed my class,
Bumped into a fence, now I'm watching grass.
I sat down to ponder, with books on my head,
But they opened up and started to spread.

'Pop quizzes' echoed in my busy mind,
I answered in rhymes, oh how I was blind!
Tests turned to riddles, and I lost my pen,
'Can I borrow yours?' asked a chicken; again!

I learned from my stumbles and midnight snacks,
Made a plan involving some silly tracks.
Like a game of hopscotch, I leapt with delight,
Learning life's lessons in chaotic flight.

So here's to the blunders that shape our days,
And the laughter that sparkles in the oddest ways.
I may be unorthodox, but I'll claim my crown,
In this circus of meaning, I won't back down!

The Elusive Echo of Clarity

I tripped on thoughts that seem to dance,
Chasing shadows, lost my chance.
With flip-flops flapping, I gallop along,
Where's that echo? It felt so wrong.

An old wise owl hoots from a tree,
"You missed your route, it's clear to me!"
But I'm too busy laughing at my fumble,
As questions jigsaw, I start to stumble.

The moon chuckles, lighting my way,
While I chase dreams that like to play.
I ask a squirrel if he's seen my mind,
He shrugs and spins; it's hard to find.

The compass spins like dizzy dancers,
Offering riddles, not second chances.
But laughter bubbles as I meander,
Trying to catch life's elusive candor.

Tardy to the Treasure Map

Woke up late with a treasure scheme,
Misread the map, oh what a dream!
X marks the spot, or so they say,
But I've found a sandwich along the way.

The compass sings, but I've lost the beat,
Pandas in tutus dance on the street.
Gold nuggets vanish like morning dew,
While I munch on chips, my crew's askew.

Pirate ghosts giggle, holding their sides,
As I bump my head, where seaweed abides.
With every misstep, I find a new quest,
Maybe the journey will be the best.

Trolling for fortune, it feels so absurd,
Laughing at life, not a single word.
So here's to treasure, both silly and grand,
Late to the party, but still joined in the band.

Fumbling for the Way Home

With a map upside down in my shaking hand,
I fumble through laughter, I don't understand.
Each corner I take leads to more surprise,
While pigeons just giggle and roll their eyes.

Wanderlust lingers, a sidewalk parade,
As I seek the light, or just delicious jade.
A cat crosses my path, smug and proud,
Is this the way home? Or am I just loud?

Street signs confuse me, they whisper and twirl,
In this funny maze, my head starts to swirl.
I trip over thoughts like loose fallen leaves,
While my friends just chuckle, what nonsense believes.

But in every tumble, I pick up a smile,
Finding fun in the chaos, it's worth the while.
So here's to the journey, wherever I roam,
With laughter and whimsy, I'll find my way home.

Minutes Slipping Through Fingers

Time's a slippery fish, there's no doubt about,
I try to catch moments, but they flail about.
I rush with a grin, racing clocks on the wall,
As seconds escape like a carnival call.

I grunt and I groan, my hair's in a twist,
What day is it now? Oh, add it to the list!
I juggle my tasks, like hot flaming pies,
While missing the point, oh how time flies!

A tortoise jogs past with a chuckle so wise,
"Slow down, dear friend, it's all in your eyes."
I pause and I giggle, the joke's on me,
As I notice the daisies, wild and free.

Minutes escape like toddlers at play,
Caught up in giggles, I'm led astray.
So here's to the chase with a wink and a sigh,
Life's fleeting moments, oh me, oh my!

The Race Against Time's Whisper

I tripped over yesterday's shoes,
Chasing dreams like a child with no clues.
Time's ticking, but I'm in slow mode,
Lost in a daze on this winding road.

The clock chuckles, spinning so fast,
While I'm here munching on breakfast at last.
A meeting with fate, I'm late for the show,
But I'll just blame the coffee's slow flow.

Steps taken with grace or a tumble,
I dance through the chaos, my thoughts all a jumble.
All these clues, they slip and they slide,
Yet I strut like a peacock, full of pride.

So here's to the chase with laughter and cheer,
Each moment I fumble, I hold dear.
In this crazy race, I'll keep in my lane,
Who cares if I stumble? I'm here for the gain!

When the Sun Sets on Decisions

The day fades out, decisions to make,
I ponder over choices, what's at stake?
Dinner's on the stove with a fierce aroma,
Yet I'm lost in thoughts of sweetened persona.

Sunset whispers, "Hurry, make a choice!"
But I'm stuck in a debate with my own voice.
Should I order pizza or whip up a stew?
Life's complex menu, I'm stuck in a queue.

A fork in the road, a literal one,
Do I cruise straight or pretend it's all fun?
With each passing minute my options grow dim,
So I grab a snack, 'cause why not on a whim?

Twilight giggles at my indecision,
While I bumble through life with a quirky vision.
With a wink and a nod, I settle for both,
As the stars appear, I finally take oath.

Sprinting Past the Unseen Signs

Round the bend, I pop like a cork,
Missed the sign flashing, "Be a little dork!"
Speeding through life on a comic book page,
With every wrong turn, I feel more sage.

I zig and I zag like a drunken bee,
While ducks quack loudly, they're judging me.
A signpost blurred by the rush of the breeze,
"Slow down," it seems to implore with unease.

In this fast lane of life, I'm losing my way,
Yet somehow I stumble upon the fun play.
With laughter and jests, I'll coast on a rhyme,
Embracing the chaos, I'll savor the climb.

So here's to unseen signs, I'll dance right through,
With a wink and a grin, to me, that's the cue.
Life's a wild race, let's throw in a laugh,
For each twist and turn adds up to my path!

Heartbeats in the Hourglass

Tick-tock goes the granter of wishes,
While I chase after dreams and tasty dishes.
Heartbeats echo in this glassy race,
As I fumble my way through this silly space.

Each grain of sand is a moment I'll flaunt,
While I trip on the edges of tasks I've fronted.
Sweeping past clocks like a whirlwind of sprites,
I juggle my thoughts amidst weathered lights.

"Hey buddy," they tease, "where's your grand plan?"
I shrug and I giggle, because life's a big tan.
With time slipping through, I gleefully stay,
Living each heartbeat like it's a cabaret.

So pour me some wine, and hand me a cheer,
As I dance with the seconds, I'm free from all fear.
In this hourglass, let joy lead the way,
For laughter and love are what make me stay!

Fleeting Gazes and Departing Trains

I missed that train, it's gone, you see,
With all my bags, I spilled my tea.
Chasing shadows, I trip and fall,
Life's a circus, and I'm the clown after all.

The clock ticks wild, a dance of haste,
I wear mismatched socks; life's a bit of a waste.
On platforms crowded, I make my stand,
Waiting for meaning, I barely understand.

A whistle blows, my chance slips by,
I wave goodbye to the passing sky.
With every step, I'm late for fate,
But with each chuckle, I celebrate.

So here I wait, let the moments play,
In this quirky race, I'll find my way.
A glimpse of purpose, perhaps tomorrow,
For now, I'll laugh, and sip my sorrow.

Sketches in the Sand

With each wave crashing, I draw a line,
But the tide laughs back; it's not so kind.
My artworks vanish as I throw a fit,
Dancing footprints lead where I don't quite fit.

Seagulls circle overhead in cheer,
Mocking my attempts, I can hear them clear.
A masterpiece here, then a slip and fall,
Life's like a beach—wild, unpredictable for all.

I scoff at the sun, too bright for my plight,
Chasing echoes of wisdom, far out of sight.
Every grain of sand a life lesson lost,
But each giggle I share, they're worth the cost.

So I sketch away while the shoreline smiles,
Creating a mess that stretches for miles.
Tomorrow I'll try, with a new plan in mind,
But today's laughter leaves worries behind.

Mornings of Unfinished Sentences

I wake up groggy, my thoughts in a flurry,
Coffee's brewing, but I'm stuck in a hurry.
A mug's half-full, just like my brain,
Words slip away, like a runaway train.

To-do lists scatter like confetti in air,
I scribble reminders, but where's my flair?
"Do not forget—" the thought fades to gray,
I laugh at my planner, who needs it anyway?

The dog won't sit, the cat steals my chair,
Each morning's a challenge, it's not quite fair.
Half of a sentence hangs in the breeze,
Life's a jigsaw with mismatched keys.

But with every hiccup, I can't help but smile,
These fragments of chaos make life worthwhile.
So here's to the mess, the laughter, the mime,
In this funny ballet, I'll bumble through time.

A Tapestry of Lost Intentions

My plans are tangled like a ball of yarn,
Each thread a dream; oops! That's a barn.
I weave my ideas into intricate patterns,
But life snips away with loud, sudden clatters.

I start to embroider, then whoops—there's a cat,
A nibble, a pounce, scratch—oh, what was that?
Intentions turn whimsical, wild and askew,
Every stitch I make comes out something new.

With colors of chaos, I thread through the days,
Losing my way in delightful malaise.
Yet every frayed edge is a story to tell,
Of laughter, of fumbles—oh, isn't that swell?

So here I gather with scissors and thread,
To make my mistakes into fabric instead.
A tapestry woven in laughter and cheer,
For life's funny journey is best when sincere.

Chasing Shadows at Dusk

In twilight's grasp, I sprint and leap,
Catching echoes that just won't keep.
With every step, the shadows tease,
   Dancing faster, put me at ease.

I stumble on thoughts, all mixed and swirled,
   Wonders of life in chaos unfurled.
   As laughter chases the fading light,
I wonder if wrong could be made right.

Barking dogs join the hurried chase,
   A funny race, a silly space.
Each fleeting moment, a jester's ploy,
While I'm left giggling, oh what a joy!

In a blur of color, the night draws near,
   I race with purpose, fueled by cheer.
   But darkness falls, my legs now sore,
What was I chasing? Who knew for sure?

The Clock Ticks Too Loud

Tick-tock, tick-tock, it starts to chime,
I swear that clock's lost all sense of time.
With a yawn and stretch, I sprint away,
But it just chuckles, while I sway.

With mismatched socks and hair askew,
I race through life like a wobbly woo.
The tick of urgency feels so benign,
Yet here I am, running out of time.

In coffee spills and awkward falls,
I tumble through the corridor walls.
Each moment laughs at my frantic pace,
As I chase meaning in this mad race.

Yet if I pause and take a look,
Maybe life's just a humorous book.
With silly plots and twists galore,
I'll read it slowly, who could ask for more?

In the Haste of Lost Moments

In the haste of too many things to do,
I trip on thoughts and dreams askew.
But what's the point of speed, I say,
If every second just slips away?

I juggle plans like clumsy clowns,
Falling hard as the laughter crowns.
Intent on grasping what slips from hand,
I find my joy has not been planned.

Around the bend, a lost sock flies,
Once a treasure, now bids goodbyes.
It rolls away to a jolly tune,
Leaving me grinning at the moon.

Moments laugh in a cosmic jest,
Perhaps the chaos is our best.
Learning to dance with the wind's sweet sighs,
Is perhaps the secret 'neath the skies.

Dashing Through the Path of Purpose

Dashing through life as if in a race,
Tripping on dreams that I can't quite chase.
Each furtive glance and frantic pout,
Makes me wonder what it's all about.

I mark my path with splatters of cheer,
While juggling tasks that seem unclear.
Each misstep invites a nursery rhyme,
Where laughter and chaos blend with time.

Fleeting moments dance as I fly by,
Chasing giggles that float like a sigh.
With purpose lost, but fun gained in score,
I'd rather crash in laughter than be a bore.

So I'll dash through the awkward and wild,
With a heart that's light and a glance beguiled.
Finding my truth in jests and jesters,
In the comedy of life, we're all the besters!

Swirling Leaves of Abandon

Chasing squirrels, I trip and fall,
My shoelaces tied in a brawl.
Leaves whirl around, a cheeky tease,
Life's little antics, oh how they please.

Hurrying on, I lose my shoe,
It's merely a sign to sit and stew.
The wind laughs hard, it's all a game,
As even time forgets my name.

A butterfly flutters, oh what a sight,
I was mindful, then lost in flight.
With every glance, my heart does race,
Yet here I am, just lost in space.

So off I go, with a jumbled thought,
To catch the sun, or a parking spot.
Life's to-do list has fallen away,
What's the rush, anyway?

Through the Window of Now

Peering through the glass so wide,
I see the chaos, my thoughts collide.
A dog in a coat, a cat in boots,
It's a circus show in my daily routes.

The clock's hands spin like a crazy top,
While I'm still here, trying to pop.
Neither here nor there, stuck in a pause,
Life's quirks hit hard, with laughter's applause.

Birds chirp gossip from branches above,
"Oh late again?" they coo with love.
I wave back, with my coffee cup,
As time takes a minute to fill me up.

With a chuckle and a munch, I forge,
Through moments that run like a wild gorge.
Oh, why rush when the world's a show?
Let's twirl in our seats, and just let it flow.

The Threads Weaving Us Apart

A needle pricked, I scream and shout,
Stitching moments, I flip about.
Life's fabric frays with each clumsy turn,
In a wild dance, I still must learn.

Intertwined threads, of joy and woe,
I patch my plans, but they always blow.
The tapestry laughs at my knotted haste,
Who knew life would be such a taste?

A fabric store's a whirlwind scene,
I choose the loud, and miss the serene.
Colors clash as I tread along,
Yet all I need is a goofy song.

With laughter's needle, I sew my fate,
In this patchwork world, it's never too late.
So I'll dance with the nonsense, spin and twirl,
And that's how I'll take on this crazy world.

Gaps in the Fabric of Hours

Tick-tock, tick-tock, the clock does tease,
I stumble over moments like autumn leaves.
Each gap in time, a funny surprise,
Like opening presents with closed eyes.

Distant echoes of laughter ring,
In a rush to catch the next big fling.
Yet humor weaves through every mishap,
A delightful trip in this cosmic map.

Horseradish thoughts stir in my mind,
I chase silly dreams that take their time.
Riding a wave of whimsical delight,
Oh, where's the hurry, let's savor the night!

So here I am, with giggles to share,
In the gaps of hours, I float in the air.
Life's impossibilities become my muse,
The joy in the chaos, my favorite ruse!

Tardy Steps on the Path

I tripped on my shoelace, lost in thought,
Chasing after wisdom that time forgot.
A squirrel scolded me for rushing along,
While I pondered if right turns are ever wrong.

The clock is ticking, or so they say,
But my feet have got other plans today.
I stopped for ice cream, it melted away,
Philosophy's sweet, but it's melting, oh, hey!

A wise old turtle said, 'Life's a race'
But I'd rather stop and enjoy the space.
With each misstep, I laugh and I sigh,
Maybe the answer's just to eat pie.

So here I am, in this comical plight,
With questions that tickle and answers in sight.
The journey's the giggle, the path full of glee,
What's lost in the chase turns to fond memory.

In Pursuit of Fleeting Moments

I missed the bus but found a sweet treat,
Life's just a buffet when you're off your feet.
With sprinkles of laughter, I chase after fun,
In the chaos of hours, I dance in the sun.

Each minute I miss just adds to my flair,
With doughnuts and coffee, I'm light as the air.
The meaning is hiding beneath all the haste,
Perhaps in my pockets I'll find a sweet taste.

As time ticks away, I sip on my drink,
Contemplating whether I'm dumb or I think.
The moments I cherish are silly and bright,
The serious stuff can wait 'til tonight.

In the whirlwind of days, I find my own pace,
Chasing giggles and grins, it's a charming race.
For every few seconds I catch and I keep,
Bring forth all the laughter and joy, that's my leap.

The Race Against Dawn

Alarm bells are blaring, what a rude wake-up!
Chased by the sun like it's all a hiccup.
I sprint down the stairs, trip on my shoe,
Wondering if caffeine can unravel this zoo.

Breakfast is flying, cereal on my head,
Do I eat or escape? Just one slice of bread.
The clock has no mercy, it's ticking away,
I chuckle at cosmos, 'You'll wait for my stay!'

The morning light giggles, it dances outside,
As I juggle my bagel and stride with pride.
Each step is a shuffle filled with comic grace,
Tangles of chaos turn into my base.

But as twilight whispers, I smile and I pause,
This race, what a joke, with its unruly laws.
I capture the moment, it's perfectly bent,
The day is a jest, and I'm fully content.

Haste of the Heart

With heart in a rush, I forgot my keys,
Tripped over my cat, fell straight to my knees.
Laughter erupts from the kitchen behind,
Even chaos can help us unwind.

I dashed out the door, a mess and a thrill,
The meaning of life took a moment to chill.
A friend on the sidewalk waved joyfully,
Caught in the whirlwind, it's just you and me.

Roadblocks and detours, we swerve and we swerve,
Each twist of the journey has its own curve.
Chasing down giggles, we dance through the fray,
What matters in life is joy on the way.

So here's to the missing and lessons we flare,
The heart of the matter is found everywhere.
In each crazy moment, we laugh and we cheer,
For truth hides within, when our hearts are sincere.

Navigating Life's Labyrinth

In a maze of choices, I race,
With signs that don't point in place.
Chasing whims, my compass spins,
Did I take a left? Or am I lost again?

Right turns and wrong, a dash to explore,
Sneaking glances at the exit door.
With every twist, I laugh and fret,
Is there a map? You know, a safety net?

Lost in thought, but it's kind of fun,
Who knew being lost could feel like a run?
Jumping through clouds of my own delight,
Maybe wandering is perfectly right!

So here's my plea to the universe wide,
Let's laugh at the chaos on this merry ride.
With a wink and a nod, I'll stumble and sway,
Life's a dance, come join the ballet!

Echoes in the Wind

Chasing whispers that tickle my ear,
I giggle aloud, what's my goal here?
The breeze carries laughter, sweet and unique,
Am I running? Or just playing hide-and-seek?

Clouds drift by with tales to impart,
I stop and ponder, do I follow my heart?
The wind just chuckles, teasing with glee,
Maybe it's best to just let it be.

In a world that spins while I look around,
I hop around like a playful hound.
With every gust comes a joyful surprise,
Life's a game, no need for goodbyes!

So I'll skip through life, carefree and bright,
With echoes that dance in the fading light.
Each moment a giggle, an echo, a spin,
In this whimsical journey, I always win!

Embracing the Uncertain Journey

Grab my hat, my shoes untied,
With a grin, I take the wild ride.
Step by step, in wobbling grace,
I chuckle at this unplanned race.

Dancing through puddles, splashes abound,
Who cares if I stumble? I'm glory-bound!
Questions like confetti, flutter and fly,
Why ask for answers? Just give it a try!

With a wink to the moon, I twirl about,
Uncertain roads are what it's about.
Through chaos and laughter, I'll take a leap,
Life's a riddle, not meant to keep.

So here's my toast to the unprepared,
With each detour, a memory shared.
Let whims guide my steps, let nonsense ensue,
Embracing the wild, I'll dance right on cue!

Time's Reluctant Embrace

Tick-tock, time plays coy,
Dancing around like a mischief toy.
I rush to meet it, but it just grins,
"Why chase the end when the fun begins?"

With seconds slipping like sand through my hand,
I reel and dart, like my own little band.
Silly plans and schemes in a whirlwind spin,
But laughter's the prize, oh, let's dive in!

Speeding past moments, I trip on my fate,
Do I have an exit? Or is it too late?
With chuckles and smiles, I'll weather the race,
And hug every minute in this wild chase.

So gather 'round, friends, let's all make haste,
Life's a banquet, no moment misplaced.
Time's a tease with a playful art,
Let's share a hug, a laugh, and a heart!

The Quickening Pulse of Reflection

I rushed past dawn, my hair a mess,
Chasing thoughts, oh what a stress.
Coffee spills on my wrinkled shirt,
  Trying to find life's secret hurt.

The dog looked up as I sprinted by,
  Probably thinks I'm a passerby.
  Did I forget my car keys too?
  Or is this life just a wild zoo?

Striding Towards Tomorrow's Questions

I jogged past wisdom, I swear it sighed,
Like a school kid who's missed the ride.
"What's the point?" the trees seem to say,
While I just chase the clouds away.

Emails pinging, I'm out of breath,
Searching for answers; does it lead to death?
Waving to squirrels, they wink and cheer,
As if they've figured it out, oh dear!

The Countdown to Nowhere

Tick-tock goes my watch, it's got no clue,
Counting down moments as if that's new.
I'm taking steps like I'm on a quest,
But where's the treasure? Just a jest!

Race against clocks, a comical dance,
Rushing through life, but never a chance.
Falling flat on my face with a grin,
Hope to find meaning beneath my skin.

Unraveled Threads of the Tapestry

Life's a tapestry, I'm pulling threads,
Patchwork of chaos, ignored my beds.
Where's the pattern? I can't quite tell,
Stitching my dreams, oh what the hell!

Colors are swirling, made quite a mess,
Who needs some order? I must confess.
A patch here, a patch there, a laugh, a sigh,
In this funny quilt, I do comply.

Unfinished Poems of the Heart

I dashed through the morning, socks askew,
Forgot my coffee, but what's a brew?
Chasing my thoughts like a wild-eyed hare,
Life's punchline hits, but I'm unaware.

The clock keeps ticking in a silly race,
Tripping on meanings, caught in a chase,
My to-do list mocks from its paper throne,
While I laugh at the chaos I call my own.

With all the wisdom of a soap dispenser,
I fumble for answers, a real life pretender,
In a world of questions, my dance is unique,
Perhaps life's key's hidden in a potato leak.

So here's to the journey, ever so spry,
With pie in my face, I'll just wave goodbye,
The heart still beats, though the rhythm's askew,
Perhaps love's the punchline, not what we pursue.

Pauses in the Pursuit of Meaning

I checked my watch—wait, what day is it?
Thoughts like balloons just won't sit and quit,
Meaning's a pinball, I'm losing my grip,
Eager for answers, but I just want to skip.

In pursuit of a treasure, I trip on my shoelace,
The map's all wonky, it's quite the disgrace,
I pause for snacks amid googling lore,
Finding out meaning's just a fast food score.

My friends all gather, and they share their tips,
With ice cream in hand, we're all taking sips,
Between bouts of laughter, we wander and roam,
It's hard to find purpose while scrolling my phone.

So here we sit, musing life's zany game,
If the search leads to laughter, is it really lame?
In the pauses we find, there's joy in the mess,
Perhaps that's the meaning—now I'll take a guess!

Lost in the Labyrinth of Life

I entered the maze with a map made of cheese,
Hoping to find clues or at least some rad peas,
Each twist and turn leaves me scratching my head,
Where's the exit? I'd settle for bread!

With every corner, I trip over fate,
The minotaur's laughing, "You're way too late!"
A riddle of laughter, I bump into walls,
The key to my life hides behind some tall balls.

I dance with the shadows, call it a jig,
Forget about purpose, let's just do a swig,
Life's like a puzzle missing key pieces,
But who needs 'em when joy never ceases?

In this goofy labyrinth, I'll stand on my groove,
With every misstep, I'm starting to prove,
That the twist that I'm on is just part of the art,
Lost isn't lost when it's fueled by the heart!

Coursing Through the Veil of Existence

Woke up this morning, my head in a haze,
Navigating life like a clumsy ballet,
The veil of existence is fragile, they say,
Yet here I am, tripping on yesterday's hay.

With all these deep thoughts, I drown in my tea,
Each sip a reminder, "Is this really me?"
The rivers of time flow right under my feet,
I'm surfing on waves, though I can't find my seat.

The veil pulls tight, like a cat with bad aim,
Each question's a puzzle, I've lost all the games,
I chase after wisdom like I chase after pies,
Only to find that I'm lost in the skies.

Yet joy's in the laughter, not found in the grind,
In moments of chaos, true freedom I find,
So I'll dance through existence, quite out of sight,
And bid the veil welcome, let's party tonight!

Intervals of Discovery

I missed the bus; how sad but bright,
Chasing thoughts like kites in flight.
With each wrong turn, I start to grin,
Life's little detours where joys begin.

Coffee spills and shoes untied,
In hasty moments, I can't decide.
A lost umbrella — oh, what a state!
But isn't this just life's fun little fate?

Maps flip-flop, directions sway,
I strut through puddles, come what may.
In this chaos, I find delight,
Who needs a plan when joy takes flight?

So here's to stumbles, slips, and slides,
As laughter rings, my heart abides.
For every mishap that I face,
Is just another dance of grace.

Timelessness in a Timed World

The clock ticks loud, but I'm unfazed,
In wrinkled clothes, I'm slightly crazed.
A rush for time but what's the prize?
I'll have a laugh while the world complies.

Calendars battle, plans go amiss,
Yet here I am, basking in bliss.
I missed my meeting, oh what a twist!
But who knew my day could be so kissed?

With every hour, I chuckle and sigh,
Embracing the chaos, oh my, oh my!
Why sprint for moments that race away?
When joy's a stroll – let's dare to play!

So here's to clocks that tick too fast,
One giggle leads to memories that last.
I'll dance with "now" while "later" waits,
In timeless laughter, I celebrate.

The Echoes of a Forgotten Call

The phone rang twice, then slipped my mind,
Voicemail blares; I'm left behind.
The message waits, a cosmic tease,
Yet I'm on the sofa, munching cheese.

A frantic search in pockets deep,
Only crayons and dreams do I keep.
Like trying to catch a runaway kite,
Life's missed calls bring such pure delight!

Text messages from the past,
Dating with urgency — what a blast!
I chuckle at plans that I evade,
A tapestry woven in mischief displayed.

So while my phone plays hide and seek,
I watch the clouds, let my heart speak.
With echoes loud, and laughter tall,
I'm answering life — I'll take it all!

Vignettes of a Stolen Minute

A stolen moment, oh what a crime,
In the rush of day, I stumble on time.
Found a penny, chased a duck,
Life's little treasures, oh so much luck.

I pause for ice cream, drips down my chin,
Not sure it's right, but I'm diving in.
Life's fast lane can wait just a while,
For sweetness savored with every smile.

In a world of deadlines, I sing a tune,
Under the clear, bright afternoon moon.
Each second I steal feels ever so bold,
Unraveling stories that never grow old.

So here's to chaos, life's big parade,
In stolen minutes, my heart's never frayed.
With laughter and whimsy guiding each part,
I find that the joy lives deep in the heart.

www.ingramcontent.com/pod-product-compliance
Lightning Source LLC
Chambersburg PA
CBHW071850160426
43209CB00003B/500